JUST JOKING

HILARIOUS DOCTOR JOKES

by Sally Lindley

WINDMILL BOOKS

Published in 2017 by Windmill Books, an Imprint of Rosen Publishing
29 East 21st Street, New York, NY 10010

Text: Sally Lindley
Illustrations: Fabio Santomauro
Design: Trudi Webb
Editors: Joe Fullman and Joe Harris

CATALOGING-IN-PUBLICATION DATA

Names: Lindley, Sally.
Title: Hilarious doctor jokes / Sally Lindley.
Description: New York : Windmill Books, 2017. | Series: Just joking | Includes index.
Identifiers: ISBN 9781508192619 (pbk.) | ISBN 9781508192558 (library bound) | ISBN 9781508192466 (6 pack)
Subjects: LCSH: Medicine--Juvenile humor. | Physicians--Juvenile humor.
Classification: LCC PN6231.M4 L563 2017 | DDC 818'.602--dc23

Manufactured in the United States of America

CPSIA Compliance Information: Batch #BS16PK: For Further Information contact Rosen Publishing, New York, New York at 1-800-237-9932

CONTENTS

Doctor! Doctor!

What did the dentist say to the golfer?

"I'm afraid you have a hole in one!"

Doctor, I keep thinking I'm Mozart!

I'll be with you in a minuet.

Doctor, I swallowed a bone.

Are you choking?

No, I really did!

What did the ninja say to the doctor?

Hi-ya!

HOW DID THE COMPUTER CATCH A COLD?

It left its Windows open!

Which is faster, hot or cold?

Hot, because anyone can catch a cold!

Why did the stand-up comedian go to see the doctor?

He was feeling a little bit funny!

Why did the snake visit the pharmacist?

It needed some asp-irin!

Doctor, first my sister was obsessed with Tangled, now she's totally into Frozen.

How long has she suffered from these Disney spells?

Why did the germ cross the microscope?

To get to the other slide!

Doctor, I feel like a well.

We must get to the bottom of this!

What did the doctor say when she delivered quadruplets?

Four crying out loud!

Doctor, I'm suffering from really bad déjà vu!

Didn't I see you yesterday?

Doctor, I keep running around pretending to be a seabird.

No wonder you're puffin!

DOCTOR, I'M SO SORRY I'M LATE, I SPRAINED MY ANKLE ON THE WAY HERE!

That's a lame excuse.

What did one toilet say to the other toilet?

You look flushed!

Did you hear about the pig that lost its voice?

It was disgruntled!

What's loud and sticky and full of germs?

A cough drop!

How do you treat an alien with claustrophobia?

Give it some space!

Doctor, I've swallowed a pen. What should I do?

Use a pencil.

WHY DIDN'T THE BOY TELL THE DOCTOR HE'D SWALLOWED SOME GLUE?

His lips were sealed!

What did the doctor say was wrong with the car mechanic?

He'd had a breakdown!

The mechanic asked for a second opinion.

"Okay," said the other doctor. "You're over-tired."

The mechanic told his wife what the doctors had said.

"Hmm," she agreed. "You do seem exhausted."

What did the doctor say to the volcano?

You need to quit smoking!

Why did the nurse tiptoe past the medicine cabinet?

He didn't want to wake the sleeping pills!

Excuse me, what's the quickest way to the hospital?

Lie down on that busy road over there!

How do you know if an aquatic mammal is ill?

They have a high beaver!

Doctor, what did the X-ray of my head show?

Absolutely nothing!

What's worse than a hippo with a cold?

A giraffe with a sore throat!

What do you give to an ailing citrus fruit?

Lemon-aid!

Doctor, I feel like a piece of cake!

Yes, you do look a bit crummy.

What can you catch but never throw?

A cold!

What award does the dentist of the year receive?

A little plaque!

Doctor, I think I need glasses.

I agree, this is a fast-food restaurant.

Why did the bee go to the doctor?

Because she had hives!

Doctor, my snoring is so bad, I'm keeping myself awake!

I think you had better sleep in another room!

Doctor, I keep comparing things with something else!

Don't panic, it's just analogy.

Who do warlocks see when they are feeling sick?

The witch doctor!

Doctor, I keep thinking I'm a bridge!

What's come over you?

A large truck and six cars!

What happened when William Shakespeare visited the doctor for his cold?

The doc said it was much achoo about nothing!

What do you give a sick pig?

Oinkment!

Did you hear about the moody dentist?

He was always looking down in the mouth!

Doctor, I have no energy. I can't even walk down the road without getting tired.

It's because you're wearing loafers!

WHY DIDN'T THE CHIMNEY FEEL VERY WELL?

It had the flue!

What did one elevator say to the other?

I think I'm coming down with something!

What did the doctor pack for her trip to the desert?

A thirst-aid kit!

What's the medical name for a fear of Santa Claus?

Claus-trophobia.

Doctor, my stomach hurts after eating crabs.

Did they smell bad when you took them out of their shells?

What do you mean "when I took them out of their shells"?

Doctor, how can I stop my nose from running?

Put your foot out, and trip it up!

WHAT DID ONE TONSIL SAY TO THE OTHER?

Dress up, the doctor is taking us out!

Did you hear about the girl who was smacked in the face by a Frisbee?

She wondered why it was getting bigger ... and then it hit her!

Why was the computer virus so serious?

It was terminal!

Doctor, I keep getting pains in my eye when I drink hot chocolate.

Have you tried taking the spoon out of your mug?

Doctor, I've painted spots all over my body.

That was a rash decision!

A sheep went to see the vet. "I feel like I always have a cloud hanging over me!"

"Ah," said the vet. "It's because you're always under the weather."

Doctor, no matter what I do, I just can't get to sleep!

Lie on the edge of the bed, and you'll soon drop off.

Doctor, I think I'm a dog!

How long have you felt like this?

Ever since I was a puppy!

How do you make a tissue dance?

Put a little boogie in it!

Doctor, I don't think these pills you gave me for heavy sweating are working.

Why not?

They keep falling out from under my arms!

Medical Mayhem!

Doctor: I'm sorry, but your son is covered in fleas and ticks.

Mother: I don't believe you.

Doctor: Why not?

Mother: They're all lice.

Doctor, I feel like a wigwam or a tepee all the time!

That just means you're two tents.

Doctor, I keep stealing things!

Hmm, have you taken anything for it?

Did you hear the joke about the germs?

I don't want you to spread it around!

Has your tooth stopped hurting yet?

I don't know, the dentist kept it.

Did you hear about the man who swallowed uranium?

He got atomic ache!

What's green and jumpy?

A frog with hiccups!

Doctor, there's a man who urgently needs you to tend to scratches all over his body.

What's his name?
Claude!

Doctor, I keep thinking I'm a mosquito.

Don't be such a sucker!

Why did the rocket visit the doctor?

To get its booster shot!

What's the Best Time to Go to the Dentist?

Tooth-hurty (2:30)!

What did the dentist say when her plane hit turbulence?

Brace yourself!

What did the boat's captain do when he was sick?

He went in to see the dock!

Doctor, I feel like a spoon.

Lie down and don't stir.

Why did the pony visit the doctor?

It was a little horse!

Why did the ninja spend a week in bed?

He had kung flu!

Doctor, how can I keep from sleepwalking?

Put thumbtacks on your bedroom floor.

Did you hear about the frog that got taken to the mental hospital?

It was hopping mad!

Did you hear about the artist who was pinned to the ground by wooden frames?

He'd come down with easels!

Did you hear about the gardener who had a cold?

He caught it from the germ-aniums!

Why did the chicken visit the doctor?

It was feeling fowl!

Doctor, my son just swallowed a roll of film.
Well, let's see if anything develops.

What did the left eye say to the right eye?
Between you and me, something smells!

What did the bucket say to the baby bucket?
You look a little pail!

DOCTOR, I KEEP THINKING I'M INVISIBLE. Who said that?

Why was there a bug in the computer?

It was looking for a byte to eat!

How do you know if you're cross-eyed?

When you can see eye to eye with yourself!

Doctor, I've got an ingrown toenail, toothache, and halitosis.

Hmm, it sounds like foot and mouth disease.

Doctor, can I get a second opinion?

Of course you can. Come back at the same time tomorrow.

What do dentists call their X-rays?

Tooth pics!

What did the nurse do when the basketball player felt sick?

She gave him the basket!

Why are the tonsils excited?

They've heard the doctor is taking them out on Friday!

Why did the ninja run around his bed?

To catch up on some sleep!

Why did the miniature tool go to see the doctor?

It was a little saw.

WHAT DO YOU CALL A SICK CROCODILE?

An illigator!

Why did the van bounce down the road?

It was a hiccup truck!

What TV shows do germs hate?

Soap operas!

What did the judge say to the dentist?

Do you swear to pull the tooth, the whole tooth, and nothing but the tooth?

How do you take a pig to the local hospital?

In a hambulance!

Doctor, I keep dreaming I'm an apple.

We need to get to the core of this.

What's green and has four legs and a trunk?

A seasick elephant!

What does the queen do if she burps?

She issues a royal pardon!

Why did the carpenter see a psychiatrist?

He had a screw loose!

Doctor, I keep thinking I'm a fish!

You poor sole.

Doctor, I think I've broken my arm in two places.

Well, don't go back there again.

Doctor, I keep thinking I'm a large ape.

OK, I'm going to need to gorilla you for some answers!

Why did the train worker get an electric shock?

He was the conductor!

What did the doctor prescribe for the pig?

Oinkment.

My dad keeps shouting out: "A! E! I! O! U!"

It sounds like he has irritable vowel syndrome.

Doctor, I keep eating nuts, bolts, and screws.

That's riveting!

How was the blind carpenter suddenly cured?

He picked up his hammer and saw!

What do you call a sick extraterrestrial?

An ailin' alien!

Doctor, I feel like a sheep.

That's baaaaad!

DID YOU HEAR ABOUT THE FROG THAT HAD A BREAKDOWN?

It got toad away!

Doctor, I feel funny.

That's hardly surprising–you look hilarious!

What's the best way to stop your nose from running?

Stand on your head!

Doctor, I really feel like a carrot, what should I do?

Well, don't get in a stew.

Doctor, I keep thinking I'm a yo-yo.

Are you trying to string me along?

A horse went to the doctor: "I sleep all day, and then I'm awake all night."

"You sound like a night-mare!"

Doctor, I keep thinking I'm a horse!

Take one of these pills every four hours, with hay.

DOCTOR, I'M REALLY AFRAID THAT I'VE TURNED INTO A VAMPIRE.

Necks, please!

Doctor, I feel like a cup of tea.

Excellent idea, make me one, too!

Doctor, I keep thinking I'm the king of the jungle.

I think you're lion.

What did the alien say when it needed blood tests?

Take me to your bleeder!

Why can't a nose be twelve inches long?

Because then it would be a foot!

Doctor, I feel like a pair of curtains.

Pull yourself together.

Did you hear about the dentist who went to the Arctic?

It was a molar expedition!

Did you hear about the truck driver with depression?

He had to pull over for a shoulder to cry on!

Doctor, I can't walk properly. I keep jumping everywhere!

Have you been feeling a bit up and down?

Why did the mummy think it had a cold?

Because of its coffin!

What did the doctor prescribe for the pony?

Cough stirrup!

The pony's cough is worse.

What do we do?

We take it to a horse-pital!

Why was the mink sent home from school?

It had a bad case of weasels!

Doctor, I think I've been put together all wrong!

Why do you think that?

Because my feet smell and my nose runs!

Doctor, my nose is all red and looks like a strawberry.

Here you go, put some cream on it.

Why did the deer visit the dentist?

He needed his buck teeth fixed!

If an athlete suffers from athlete's foot, what does a soldier suffer from?

Missile-toe!

Doctor: You need new glasses.

Patient: How do you know?

Doctor: I could tell as soon as you walked through the window.

Which subject did the dentist get an A in at school?

Flossophy!

Doctor, I think I'm becoming invisible.

Yes, I can see that you're not all there.

Hospital Hilarity!

Doctor, I've lost my memory!

When did that happen?

When did what happen?

What did the sailor say as he threw up on a windy day?

It's all coming back to me now!

What can run but can't walk?

Your nose!

Doctor, my monkey doesn't like his medicine.

Tell him he'll get what he's gibbon.

Why did the teacher visit the optician?

She couldn't control her pupils!

What do you get if you cross a comedian and germs?

A sick joke!

What do you call a pig lying in the Sun?

Bacon!

Doctor, everyone keeps ignoring me.

Next, please!

DOCTOR, I THINK I'M A BELL. WHAT SHOULD I DO?

Take this medicine, and if nothing changes, give me a ring!

Did you hear the joke about bad breath?

It stinks!

Did you hear about the man who was hit on the head by an icicle?

It knocked him cold!

Doctor, I keep thinking I'm a nit.

Will you please get out of my hair?

What do you give sick insects?

Anty-biotics

DOCTOR, HELP! I THINK I'M SHRINKING!

Wait there, and be a little patient.

Why did the computer sneeze?

Because it had a virus!

What does a doctor give to an elephant with a vomiting bug?

Plenty of room!

Did you hear about the frog with the broken leg?

It was feeling unhoppy!

Doctor, I keep thinking I'm a caterpillar.

Don't worry, you'll soon change.

What did the doctor say to the sick bodybuilder?

Take a seat in the weighting room.

DOCTOR, I KEEP THINKING I'M A WASP!

Buzz off, and stop bothering me!

What happens when you can't find a bathroom?

Urine for the duration.

Did you hear about the thief who went to the doctor because she couldn't sleep?

The doctor gave her a mat and told her to lie low for a while.

Where do people get their medicine in the countryside?

From a farmer-cist!

Doctor, I keep thinking I'm a spider.

Sounds like a web of lies to me.

Why did the carpenter visit the doctor?

He had a window pain!

Doctor, I keep hearing a ringing sound!

Then answer your phone, silly!

When does a doctor get angry?

When she runs out of patients!

Astronaut: How can I get my baby to sleep?

Doctor: Rocket!

Doctor, I think I'm a rubber band.

Just stretch yourself out on the couch, and tell me all about it.

Why did the pie go to the dentist?

It needed a filling!

Doctor, everything I touch turns to gold!

Don't worry, it's just a gilt complex.

Why did the banana go to see the doctor?

Because it wasn't peeling well!

What's the best cure for graphite poisoning?

Pencil-lin!

A man goes to see the doctor. He has a cucumber in one ear, a breadstick in the other ear, and a banana up his nose. The doctor knows instantly what is wrong.

"You're not eating properly!"

What's a dentist's top attraction at the amusement park?

The "fluor-ride!"

Why did the dentist keep falling asleep?

Because drilling teeth is boring!

Why was the doctor worried about the obese alien?

It was an extra-cholesteroll!

Why do you feel down in the mouth when you have a cold?

Because your nose is off-scenter!

What did the doctor give to the nervous elephant?

A pill to make him trunkquil!

Did you hear about the witch who turned green?

She got broom sick on long journeys!

Doctor, I keep thinking that I'm a dog!

Climb up on the couch, and I'll take a look at you.

But I'm not allowed on the couch!

Doctor, would you say I have a split personality?

One at a time, please!

Doctor, everyone thinks I'm a liar.

I can't believe that!

DID YOU HEAR ABOUT THE PIG THAT WENT ON A PLANE?

Swine flu!

My mother's a dreadful dancer. She has two left feet.

My mother's like that, too. The doctor told her to wear flip-flips.

How do psychiatrists greet each other?

You are fine. How am I?

Doctor, I'm so confused. Please help me out!

Certainly, the door is there on your left.

Doctor, the Invisible Man is here for his appointment.

Tell him I can't see him now.

Doctor, I keep seeing an insect circling my head.

Don't worry. That's just a bug that's been going around.

WHY DID THE CLOWN CALL THE DOCTOR?

Because he broke his funny bone!

Why did the king visit the dentist?

To get his teeth crowned!

Doctor, I always dream there are monsters under the bed.

Saw the legs off the bed, and you'll be fine!

Doctor, I keep thinking I'm an electric eel.

That's shocking!

Doctor, I dreamed last night that I'd turned into a deck of cards.

I'll deal with you later!

Why did the dalmation go to the eye doctor?

It kept seeing spots!

What did the dermatologist say to the frog?

People will learn to love you, warts and all!

Doctor, I keep thinking I've turned into a frog.

What's so bad about that?

I'm afraid I might croak!

Doctor, I think I'm an introverted snail.

Don't worry, we'll soon bring you out of your shell.

What noise did the train make when it had a cold?

Aaaa-choo-choo!

Why did the doctor send the vampire to the nurse?

For blood tests!

When should you go to see a bird doctor?

When you're puffin!

Doctor, my brother thinks he's an escalator.

Tell him to come and see me.

I can't, he doesn't go up to this floor.

What did the doctor give to the bird with a sore throat?

Tweetment!

WHAT DID THE LITTLE BROOM SAY TO THE BIG BROOM?

I just can't get to sweep!

Why did the duck visit the doctor?

It thought it was quacking up!

What did the doctor say to the patient after surgery?

That's enough out of you!

Doctor, I keep getting pins and needles.

Yes, I can see your point.

A librarian went to see a nurse after being hit on the head by some books.

She's only got her shelf to blame.

Doctor, I keep thinking I'm a moth.

Will you get out of my way, you're in my light!

DID YOU HEAR ABOUT THE BEAR THAT ENDED UP IN A HOSPITAL?

It had a grizzly accident!

What did the doctor give to the scientist with bad breath?

Experi-mints!

Doctor, everyone keeps disagreeing with me.

No, they don't!

Doctor, I keep seeing spots!

Have you seen a doctor?

No, just spots.

Why did the teddy bear visit the doctor?

It felt all stuffed up!

Doctor, will this cream get rid of my itching?

Well, I don't want to make any rash promises!

What do you call a pig with no legs?

A groundhog!

Which animals make the best dentists?

Molar bears!

Have you seen the website conjunctivitis.com?

It's a site for sore eyes!

Did you hear about the man who swallowed his money?

The doctor was looking for signs of change.

Further Reading

Chmielewski, Gary. *The Medical Zone.* Norwood House Press, 2014.

MacIntyre, Mickey. *The Really Funny Doctor! Doctor! Joke Book For Kids.* Bell & Mackenzie, 2014.

McCourt, Richard, and Dominic Wood. *Dick and Dom's Big Fat and Very Silly Joke Book.* Macmillan Children's Books, 2014.

Glossary

booster shot A second dose of a vaccine given in order to strengthen or "boost" the first dose.

claustrophobia An extreme fear of confined or closed-in spaces.

déjà vu The feeling that you've experienced something before.

pharmacist Someone who is officially allowed to dispense and sell drugs.

uranium A substance used to make atomic bombs.

Index